REAL CHANG

MOR

POWE ᴰ᥆᥆ION

UNDERSTAND. MEASURE. TRAIN.

by Christina Ricci
LPGA CLASS A
TPI GOLF 3 & POWER LEVEL 2
CROSSFIT LEVEL 2
BEST-SELLING GOLF AUTHOR

featuring
Nick Antonelli

Illustrations by Robyn Neild, UK
Edited by Mike Kennedy

References:
Titleist Performance Institute - mytpi.com
Trackman.com stats and data used with permission

Volume discounts available. Visit getmorepars.com to learn more or register
for wholesale pricing (Retailers and Golf Industry Professionals). Please email
inquiries to: hello@christinariccigolf.com

ISBN 978-0-9793469-83

Printed in China

MORE PARS!
POCKET GUIDE COLLECTION

Each guide is jam-packed with Christina's signature style of
YES/NOs, STEP 1-2-3s and easy-to-follow, re-creatable
visuals. Each Guide comes with its own button-snap clear
envelope. The perfect event welcome gift. Quantity
discounts auto-applied during checkout.

www.GetMorePars.com

ACKNOWLEDGMENTS

Golf is an incredible opportunity to meet amazing people from all over the world. I feel fortunate to have high-energy passion to help others achieve their goals through my books and camps. I cannot do all this alone. It takes a team to produce successful camps and golf books. This book is extra special with the inclusion of Nick Antonelli! Nick is an exceptional player and coach. I am confident that you will truly enjoy learning from his incredible technique. A very special thank you to Atkinson Resort & Country Club, Renaissance Country Club and Reunion Resort & Spa for their support. When embarking on the creation of a new book, I write many-many pages. Oftentimes, 1000+ pages! It is not an easy task to edit for the printed edition. The other pages become my digital collection. A big thank you goes out to Mike Kennedy for his meticulous edits. An avid player himself, he stated after he completed his work. *"I have to admit that while I was proofing these books, I'd get up about every 10 minutes and try something that I just read. Any improvement in my game this year automatically gets credited to you!"* A thank you to JT Dowd for his equipment expertise, Crossfit Full Potential, my good friend Phil for his unyielding encouragement, Duke Butler for his friendship and words of wisdom (p 25) and as always, my Mom for her loving support.

4

follow Nick on
instagram
@antonelligolf

ACKNOWLEDGMENTS PASSION & GRATITUDE

MORE ABOUT NICK

Nick Antonelli picked up the stick at a very young
age. He is a former member of the PGA Tour
Canada (now called Mackenzie Tour) and Trackman
Certified. He enjoys helping players of all ages and
ability levels with all facets of their game. He
shoots in the high 60's and is looking forward to
introducing his young daughter to the game.

CHRISTINA RICCI IS LPGA CLASS A, TPI GOLF LEVEL 3 &
POWER LEVEL 2 CERTIFIED, CROSSFIT LEVEL 2 AND A
BEST-SELLING GOLF AUTHOR.

Christina took up the game in 2000 and dropped to a 5
handicap in five short years. She published her first book,
A Girl's On-Course Survival Guide to Golf in 2008 and never
looked back. She has authored five books and 20 pocket
guides, sells branded golf accessories, hosts national golf
camps, and teaches locally at the beautiful Atkinson
Resort & Country Club located in Atkinson New
Hampshire, 45 minutes north of Boston. She's been

featured on the cover of *GolfTips* magazine and her popular golf tips are featured on the Golf Channel, her YouTube Channel (youtube.com/c/morepars), and online portals such as WomensGolf.com, Golfforher.com and LPGA Women's Network.

AS SEEN ON THE
GOLF CHANNEL

"Christina Ricci is a trailblazer in golf. She has introduced tens of thousands of players to the game utilizing her successful methodologies coupled with her keen knowledge and upbeat spirit. Whether it's a video, camp or a teaching segment on the Golf Channel, Ricci resonates with her students in a powerful, yet relatable way."

- Emmy Moore Minister,
Board Member and Past President
Women in the Golf Industry

WOMEN IN THE GOLF INDUSTRY
powered by connections

WHAT THIS GUIDE IS, WHAT IT IS NOT, AND HOW TO USE IT

This guide is your go-to for understanding, measuring and training for more distance off the tee and from the fairway. It is divided into three core sections:

1. POWER BODY
2. POWER TECHNIQUE
3. POWER EQUIPMENT

Within each section you'll first learn the whys. It is important to **understand** the general principles and concepts before applying them to your game. Knowledge is power. It is my opinion that golf handicaps have not changed because of this. Students do as their instructors ask or watch YouTube videos. But oftentimes, they do not truly understand the core principles of the golf swing in relation to their body, equipment and technique. In addition, I see far too many players misdiagnosing themselves, which sends them down the wrong path. Instead, let's truly educate you on the

look for these helpful icons along the way

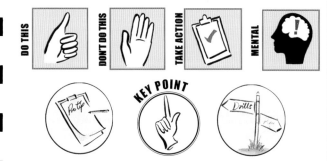

DO THIS

DON'T DO THIS

TAKE ACTION

MENTAL

Pro Tip

KEY POINT

Drills
Play

essentials of ball striking so you can experience real change in your game.

You'll **measure** your current body, equipment and technique for an accurate starting point. From there, you'll apply new knowledge of skills with **training**. This Guide is not a replacement for your instructor. I highly recommend working with a coach or training through the MorePars.com platform. The best players in the world have swing, fitness and/or medical coaches. As recreational players, you too can train like the pros and experience significant gains off the tee and from the fairway. Are you ready for more power and pars? **Let's get to it!**

Understand. Measure. Train. **MORE PARS!**

NEXT STEPS **TO MORE PARS**

I encourage you to explore the ***More Pars Training*** series. Step-by-step, actionable booklets with optional remote coach engagement. Visit **MorePars.com** to explore packages with Christina and comprehensive self-guided video courses.

ON THE GREEN TRAINING

Getting really good on the green is the fastest path to more pars, yet few train for putting. *Are you ready for less putts?*

SHORT GAME TRAINING

Many players struggle with short shots around the green. Why? Confusion with conceptuals, set-up, technique and strategy end up resulting in a mean game of pinball. *Are you ready for more up & downs?*

POWER TRAINING

There is no cookie-cutter swing, but there are essential keys to optimize center-face contact and efficiency of power. *Are you ready for lots more distance?*

LONG GAME TRAINING

This More Pars Training focuses on your long game from the fairway. Our goal is solid, long and accurate for more GIRs. *Are you ready for more greens in regulation?*

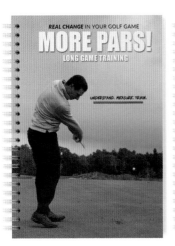

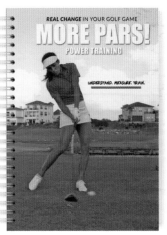

Step by step how-to guides for actionable training!

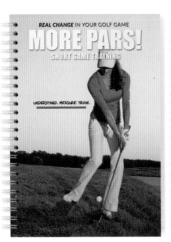

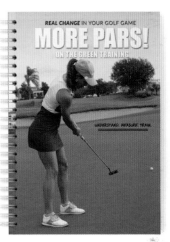

Contents

SECTION I POWER BODY

POWER, STRENGTH, SPEED & MOBILITY ASSESSMENTS

SECTION II POWER TECHNIQUE

a smashed ball is a happy ball

13

Contents

POWER LEAKS
SWING CHARACTERISTICS & FIXES

MORE DISTANCE
GET THE DISTANCE YOU WANT

STRATEGIES FOR
PHYSICAL LIMITATIONS

*MP - Head to MorePars.com to view this
section of the book! Plus, every section
includes extended pages. View online!

Contents

SECTION III POWER EQUIPMENT

NEXT STEPS
MorePars.com **Use promo code** book
for 10% discount on membership!

HI! I'M CHRISTINA!

First and foremost, welcome! I am thrilled to have the opportunity to help you achieve more distance and power in your golf game. Golf is a demanding sport, both physically and mentally. It demands our full attention to be great. I think we can agree that hitting the ball really far is great too! Plus, it makes the game easier. In order to get that distance, there are three core modules that work as a team to get you big distance:

- BODY
- EQUIPMENT
- TECHNIQUE

These three modules (defined further on next pages) along with your game goals will pave a path to achieving significant gains in your distance off the tee and from the fairway.

My goal during your Power Training is to optimize your:

- BALL SPEED
- SMASH-FACTOR
- SPIN RATE

Most importantly, as you complete each section within this extensive More Pars Power series, you'll **understand** the whys, **measure** your game, and **train** for more power...and more pars.

Christina Ricci
Your More Pars Coach

So, let's get to it!

LPGA CLASS A
TITLEIST PERFORMANCE INSTITUTE GOLF LEVEL 3
POWER LEVEL 2, CROSSFIT LEVEL 2

19

POWER TRAINING

1. BODY
2. TECHNIQUE
3. EQUIPMENT

Three Power Training Modules work together as a team to produce more distance and solid ball striking. If one of these modules is not up to par, the others will be forced to scramble. By optimizing all three, you'll experience significant gains in distance, more accuracy and lots more pars. ***Understand. Measure. Train!***

POWER **BODY** Your body is designed to output tremendous power, *if you train for it.* What can your body produce for power today? Knowing this is paramount for change tomorrow.

UNDERSTAND THE WHYS.

POWER **TECHNIQUE** Players who go long on the PGA Tour often only have a wedge into the green. They rake in the money. As recreational players, we can adopt their power techniques, such as optimizing the kinematic sequence for an efficient and powerful swing.

MEASURE YOUR POWER.

POWER **EQUIPMENT** Optimizing your equipment parameters such as length, lie, loft, flex, and CG profile are very important. Your shoes, grips and apparel play a key role as well.

TRAIN FOR POWER.

5 TIPS **FOR SUCCESS**

TIP NO. 1 **ASK QUESTIONS**

When I was learning, my instructor always said
the only dumb question is the one that you do
not ask. We'll be covering lots of techniques
and golf skills during our time together. With
that, you may get confused, perplexed and

FACT:
There is no such
thing as muscle
memory.

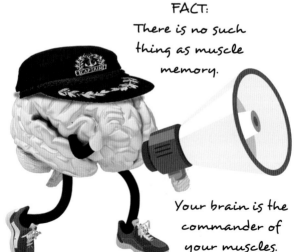

Your brain is the
commander of
your muscles.

22

bewildered...that's expected and perfectly okay. If I didn't understand a concept, I would ask the instructors to please clarify. We all learn differently and sometimes, as an instructor, we need to phrase our directives so that you as the student get it.

TIP NO. 2 STAY FOCUSED

As you are grooving techniques that I, through this book or the MorePars.com platform, or your coach present to you, it is important to stay focused on these specific tasks. They are designed to build a foundation for your golf skill set. If you deviate with a million other thoughts that you may have read or heard, then chances are the principles will not stick. Our brains are wired to only store what we focus on...so stay focused!

TIP NO. 3 SHELVE THE SELF DIAGNOSIS

With the easy accessability to YouTube and other
video golf sites, it is tempting to self-diagnose your
swing issues. You may be accurate with your
diagnosis…and you may not. Misdiagnosing can
lead to new swing woes. Instead, let your coach
diagnosis and prescribe the solution for you.

24

TIP NO. 4 **SWING THOUGHTS ON-COURSE**

Limit your swing thoughts to one or two at a time, especially while playing. Your brain needs time to process and re-wire new techniques. Your brain also needs constant reinforcement, so rehearse these new skills often. Your goal is to store your new skill set into your long-term memory bank! Overloading with thoughts will delay progress.

WHAT YOU PERCEIVE YOU CAN ACHIEVE. DREAM, DARE AND DO!

TIP NO. 5 **TRY LESS!**

If I had to say what would be the best tip? Try less! We comprehend more when we are relaxed and having fun, not trying hard. When we try hard, we tense up. Tense muscles are slow muscles. While we're at it...let's eliminate the word *try* from our golf vocabulary. It's non-committal. Let's replace it with:

Let's do this!

POWER BODY

Inside this section

What is Power?
What's Your Engine?
Understanding Your Muscles
How We Train Golf Power
Power & Strength Assessments
Mobility & Stability Assessments

In this section, we will focus on the most important piece of equipment. Your body! It is designed to provide tremendous power, if you train for it. The first step is to understand what your body can produce for power at this moment in time. We'll begin with a series of Power Assessments to establish a baseline. We'll also look under the hood to determine what kind of car you drive with a trip back to childhood.

From there, we'll dive into understanding our muscles. Our bodies are intricate systems with a Central Nervous System (CNS) in the driver's seat.

Like the turtle, Type I muscles are not capable of big power.

And when it comes to generating power, the CNS needs to command a specific type of muscle called Type IIx. Type IIx are explosive muscles. They can provide quick bursts of energy (i.e. sprinters). This type of muscle, however, fatigues quickly. Another muscle type is called Type I. These are our everyday and endurance muscles. They are slower to fatigue. (i.e. marathon runners).

Inside this Power Body module, you'll learn how to call on these muscles and how to build more.

So, let's get to it!

WHAT IS POWER?

FORCE x VELOCITY = POWER

The rate at which you produce a force—strong and fast—equals power. As golfers, applying this equation can produce incredible distance gains. The first step is to understand what power is. The second is to train our bodies to produce that rate of force—on demand.

Force is created by muscles, which is why we need strength. Strength alone cannot produce speed. Speed alone cannot produce force. We need strength + speed to get power.

WE NEED STRENGTH + SPEED FOR
MAXIMUM POWER OUTPUT

HOW DOES POWER RELATE TO
GOLF?

In order to get better, we need to train specifically for golf, both physically and mentally. Let's first talk fitness and how it relates to the game. Would you agree that:

GOLF IS A SPORT? GOLF IS PHYSICAL? IT REQUIRES HIGH VELOCITY ENERGY?

Bravo if you answered yes to all of these questions! The golf swing is very demanding of our bodies. It requires positions that are athletic and torqued up. From that torqued position, golf asks us to move the club at warp speed to generate max ball speed. The more we train specifically for power, the easier it is to generate max velocity for mega distance. A de-conditioned

body will struggle to maintain good technique and could possibly cause injury in a passionate effort to manufacture power. Unfortunately, the results are not always optimal. The good news is that by UNDERSTANDING the whys of your BODY, EQUIPMENT and TECHNIQUE, you'll be well-equipped to create real change and real power for your game.

WHY

IS POWER SO IMPORTANT?

Long hitters on the PGA Tour—such as Brooks
Koepka, Dustin Johnson, Jon Rahm, Justin
Thomas and Tiger Woods—average 300+
yards on their drives and are consistently Top
10 finishers. Same deal with the LPGA Tour.
Players such as Lexi Thompson, Brittany
Lincicome, Karrie Webb, Nelly Korda and
Laura Davies make their game easier with
longer balls. Instead of a 5-iron or 3-wood in,
long ball hitters are using a short iron or
wedge. Not only that, hitting the ball really
far is empowering and more fun.

DISTANCE MAKES THE GAME EASIER.

DISTANCE TROPHY

WHO WOULD **YOU** RATHER BE?

Id rather hit
it really far!

I prefer
accuracy.

WHAT'S YOUR
ENGINE?

LET'S FIND OUT

What sports did you play growing up
and at what age did you start?

Which did you or do you prefer:
sprinting or distance runs?

Did you or do you play any
hand/eye sports?

Did you or do you play any team sports,
and at what level?

Do you play any sports outside of golf?

What do you do for general fitness?

What is your intensity level when you
train? (1 = Sunday Drive or 10 = Rush Hour)

LET'S HEAD BACK TO CHILDHOOD

Believe it or not, what you did in your childhood applies to your athletic potential as an adult. If you played sports as a kid such as baseball, softball, tennis, hockey, football, or track, then chances are you developed a good number of Type IIx muscle

fibers. Type IIx are utilized for short bursts of speed and power. Type I or endurance muscles are

Playing a variety of sports as a child has significant benefits for your golf game. I ran track, and played tennis, field hockey, softball and basketball.

slower to fatigue. These are our everyday muscles. Type I are much like a turtle. They just keep going and going. Long distance runners use Type I muscles.

Just like the hare, Type II are fast-twitch muscles. As we age, Type II muscles decrease in

While learning the violin won't train your Type IIx muscles, it will develop the right side of your brain, which is where we should play golf.

availability (they disappear). However, if they are trained, they can increase. So if you did not participate in many sports growing up, or even if you did, you still have an opportunity to build Type IIx muscles. You can then call on them for your golf game. Actually, we need both muscle types to play great golf. Type I fibers produce less force, but they are able to maintain longer-term contractions, key for stabilization and postural control. If you're a player interested in more distance, then you must incorporate power training into your lifestyle. Don't be scared. You'll discover that it is the best thing you ever did for your game and your body.

GOLF'S ENGINE

Golf Power Training incorporates four major sources in the body: Vertical, Rotary, Chop and Wrist Power. As you train, Vertical, Rotary, Chop and Wrist Power, you are essentially training your central nervous system to call on more muscle fibers, specifically your larger muscle fibers that produce explosive power for your golf swing.

TAKE ACTION

Visit MorePars.com to learn more about Power Training programs - live anywhere.

UNDERSTANDING
YOUR MUSCLES
HOW THEY ARE CREATED

Muscles are created by the workouts that we do.
Muscles are made up of fibers, lots and lots of
them. Based on what we are asking our muscles to
do, the command center—
the Central Nervous
System—will send the
appropriate signals to get
the job done. For example,
if you're simply picking up
a piece of paper that fell on
the floor, that's not going
to require a large
recruitment of muscle fibers.

Muscle fibers

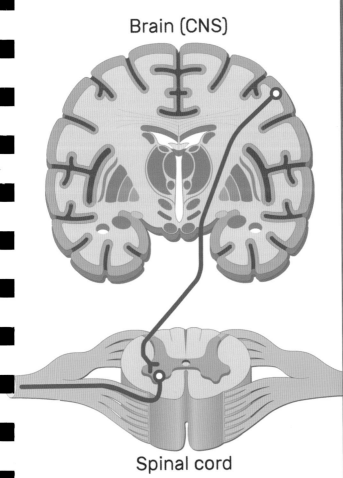

Brain (CNS)

Spinal cord

IT'S ALL ABOUT THE EXERTION AND INTENSITY. THAT'S WHERE THE MAGIC IS.

But if you are pushing a heavy sled up a hill, you better believe the CNS is going to call all the troops to get in on this action to help you get the job done. So the more we call on the large muscle units, the more we are training the Type II muscles. But again, we need to specifically train for this with strategy and customization based on your goals and your body.

WHAT DOES PULLING A SLED HAVE TO DO WITH GOLF?

Training outside of golf with intensity—exerting our muscles with a mix of speed and strength—trains our Central Nervous System to fire faster and recruit more muscle fibers. It doesn't matter what sport, as long as you are training the motor units.

Another great application of the Type IIx is
the fight or flight. Imagine that a tiger is
chasing you. Yikes! Type II's to the rescue.
You'll feel an explosive burst of energy, like a
Marvel comics character, so you run for your
life. These are the same muscles we need in
our golf game. But here's the deal, this type
of energy only lasts about 10 seconds and
fatigues quickly. The good news, you'll have
an entire hole to restore this energy.

FIGHT OR FLIGHT

TRAINING  4 MODULES

FOR GOLF POWER

VERTICAL POWER

Many PGA Tour
players jump
3-4 inches and
the long-driver
hitters 5+ (inches)
through impact. Vertical
thrust creates tremendous
explosive power and lots of
distance.

VERTICAL
POWER

Head to
MorePars.com
to explore this
section!

ROTARY POWER

The speed at which we rotate our body segments and in what order (Kinematic Sequence).

CHOP POWER

In the golf swing, Chop Power refers to the force and speed of your arms from the top of your backswing and then down and through to your lead side. Long drive hitters are 50 percent faster with their thorax to arm speed than the PGA Tour players!

WRIST POWER

Our wrists can move in 3-dimensional planes. The best players use these planes to create incredible wrist speed.

POWER, STRENGTH, SPEED & MOBILITY ASSESSMENTS

TAKE ACTION

As a MorePars.com member, you'll have access to lots of Power Body resources to support your training.

WELCOME TO POWER, STRENGTH, SPEED & MOBILITY ASSESSMENTS.

This module is designed to evaluate YOU, your most important piece of equipment. A stable and flexible body will provide a solid foundation in which to build strength and speed. We cannot output power with just strength...or just speed. We need both. To get the most from the Power Body Module, head to MorePars.com. As a member, you'll gain access to videos that support every assessment presented, evaluation sheets, and direct coaching from Christina with More Pars VIP packages. The next few pages provide a general overview of these assessments. *So, let's get to it!*

GEAR FOR ASSESSMENTS

- Medball that is 5% of your body weight
- Tape measure
- Cones (or similar)
- Chair
- Cable machine
- Dumbbells
- Mat
- Racquetball
- Shaft
- Pen

TAKE ACTION

JUST LIKE ON THE COURSE, IT IS CRITICAL TO **UNDERSTAND** WHERE YOU ARE LOSING YOUR STROKES.

TAKE ACTION

Head to MorePars.com to watch instructional videos and perform the Power Body Assessments.

POWER
ASSESSMENTS

Let's identify your power strengths and leaks within your body to understand where you are losing power.

CHEST THROW
Measures upper body (chest /triceps) and core power

SIT-UP &THROW
Measures core and lat power

VERTICAL JUMP & BROAD JUMP
Measures leg and core power

SHOT PUT
Measures core body strength, symmetry and total body power

To generate power, we need the combination of strength + speed. A solid base of strength helps to stabilize and control the forces of the golf swing.

STRENGTH ASSESSMENTS

SPLIT SQUAT

Measures ability to stabilize and generate ground force

CABLE PRESS - SINGLE ARM

Measures ability to move force away from the body

CABLE PULL- SINGLE ARM

Measures ability to move force toward the body

PUSH UP

Measures upper body strength

GRIP STRENGTH

Measures isometric strength of the hand and forearm muscles

SPEED & COORDINATION ASSESSMENTS

15 FOOT SHUTTLE

Measures explosive speed and ability to recover

SWISH TEST

Measures speed on dominant and non-dominant sides

WALL TOSS

Measures symmetry and hand/eye coordination

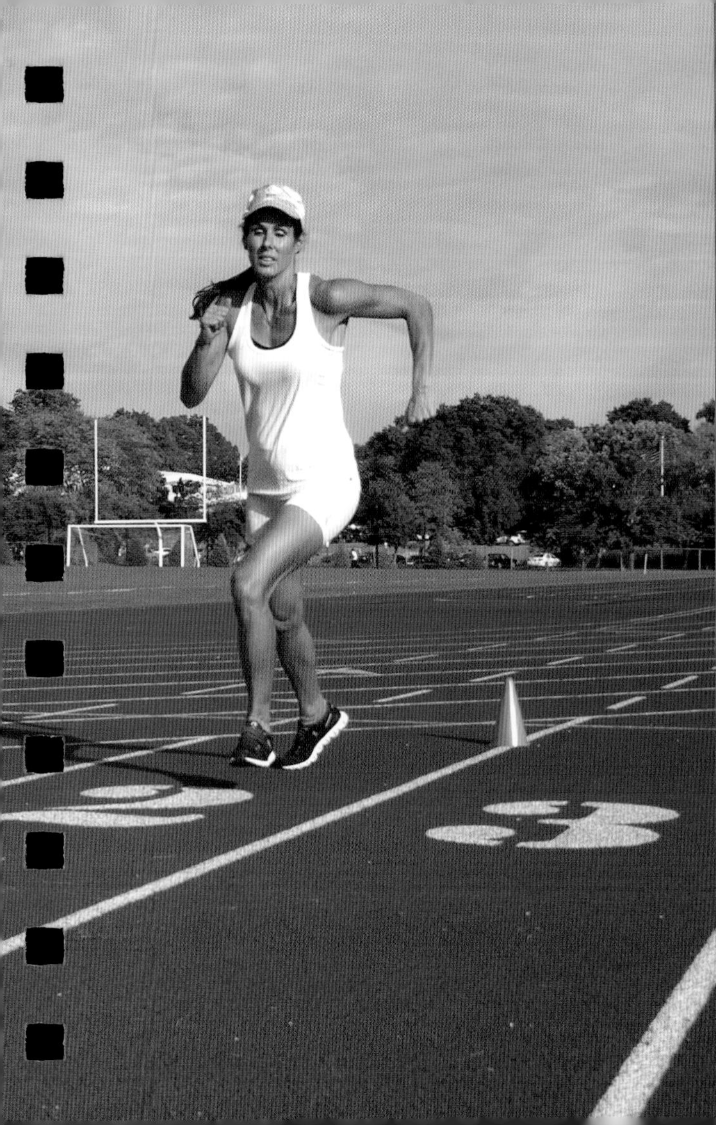

MOBILITY & STABILITY
ASSESSMENTS

Mobility and stability assessments are the very first steps to determine your overall mobility and stability. Once reviewed, your More Pars Coach will prescribe the appropriate exercises

 for you. Head to More Pars to view detailed instructions on how to perform these tests, as well as to download a mark sheet.

TAKE ACTION

POWER
TECHNIQUE

Inside this section

Ball Laws
Get Your Desired Ball Flight
Get More Distance
Power Leaks & Fixes
Power Modifications
Physical Limitations

In this section, we will focus on the mechanics of the golf swing. Our goal is to help you design an efficient and powerful swing that you can call on demand. Everyone has their own unique swing engine. There is no cookie-cutter swing. However, there are essential keys to the golf swing that you must optimize to maximize distance and accuracy. Maximizing distance, makes the game easier. We'll focus on optimizing your clubhead speed, impact point and attack angle. Optimizing these will produce max ball speed, an optimal launch angle and ideal spin rate for *your* swing.

Understanding why the ball flies and travels the way it does is also a critical component. Terms you'll learn are launch direction and curve, face-to-path, launch angle, spin rate, smash-factor, and the relationship between ball and clubhead speed. Combining these factors in an optimal way will help you to maximize your distance! As with all the Power modules, we'll get baseline assessments to determine a starting point. The object of the game is to get the ball to your intended target, tee to green. The more times you can do that, the more consistent you'll be.

So, let's get to it!

UNDERSTANDING
BALL LAWS

Knowing why the ball does what it does just after the point of impact is critical. We call these ball laws. There are four factors that you need to understand to be a better player...and a better student. Also understanding that golf is a numbers game and by optimizing your numbers in degrees, you'll increase your numbers in yards.

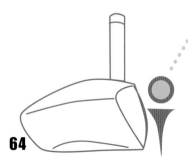

4 factors that you as a golfer can control through your technique

1. LAUNCH DIRECTION & CURVE

Does the ball start left of target, on target, or right of target?

Does it have a curvature to its flight?

2. LAUNCH ANGLE

How high or low is the ball flight?

3. SPIN RATE

How fast is the ball back-spinning?

4. BALL SPEED

How fast is the ball moving from point A to point B?

LEARN THE
WHYS

1. WHY DOES THE BALL START THAT WAY?

2. WHY DOES THE BALL CURVE?

3. WHY DID THE BALL GO THAT DISTANCE?

Understanding the relationship of your club's face and your club's path is the very first step to understanding why the ball started on that line. Understanding the impact of where on the clubface you make contact is also very important. The areas that we will discuss are Launch Direction and Launch Angle, and what you can do to optimize them.

A COMMON
STUDENT
SCENARIO

IT'S MY ALIGNMENT!

Susan says to me, "Christina, all my balls off the tee are going left. Our course is tight so many of my balls are ending up in the rough or woods. I think it's my alignment, so I have been aiming more right to fix it. The problem, though, it's getting worse. Can you help?"

"Yes, Susan. I am happy to help you! My guess is that it's not your alignment, but your launch direction that is most likely the culprit."

"What's that?," Susan asks looking perplexed.

Susan needs to learn the whys. Why did the ball start where it did? Why did it curve? Why'd it go that far? One reason could indeed be her alignment, which is why a comprehensive assessment is critical to determine Susan's baseline technique.

LAUNCH DIRECTION & CURVE

In a perfect world, what would you like to see your ball do when it comes off the face? Would it curve or stay straight? How far would it fly in the air? How far would it roll once landing? Understanding what you want and how to get it is very empowering. The first step is to understand. The second is to assess your current ball flight pattern.

THERE ARE 13 BALL FLIGHTS, 3 START LINES AND 3 SHOT SHAPES.

TAKE ACTION

Set up a noodle station to determine your start direction. Head to the *How to Change Ball Flight* Section.

72

LAUNCH DIRECTION

3 } START LINES

BALLS CAN START:

1. Left of the target
2. Right of the target
3. On the target line

3}

FLIGHT SHAPES

BALLS CAN:

1. Curve left to right
2. Curve right to left
3. Stay straight on target line

13

BALL FLIGHTS

STARTS LEFT OF TARGET LINE

1. PULL HOOK
2. PULL
3. PULL FADE
4. PULL SLICE
5. FADE

STARTS ON THE TARGET LINE

1. SLICE
2. HOOK
3. STRAIGHT

PLAYABLE BALL FLIGHT: ENDS UP AT THE TARGET

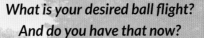

What is your desired ball flight?
And do you have that now?

STARTS RIGHT OF TARGET LINE

Of those 13, only 3 are considered playable ball flights because they end up at the target. (highlighted in orange)

1. PUSH SLICE

2. PUSH

3. PUSH DRAW

4. PUSH HOOK

5. DRAW

SPIN AXIS

WHAT CAUSES THE BALL TO CURVE?

A SPIN AXIS BETWEEN -2 AND 2 CAN BE CONSIDERED A STRAIGHT SHOT

NO CURVE

0°

0°

**0°
SPIN AXIS**

Zero spin axis, and the plane
would fly straight.

**+ POSITIVE
SPIN AXIS**

Positive spin axis, and the plane
would curve to the right.

Let's use an airplane as an example for spin axis. If the wings of an airplane are parallel to the ground, this would represent a zero spin axis and the plane would fly straight. If the wings were tilted to the left (right wing higher than left wing), this would represent a negative spin axis and the plane would tilt to the left. And the opposite holds true if the wings are tilted to the right.

- NEGATIVE SPIN AXIS

Negative spin axis, and the plane
would curve to the left.

GEAR EFFECT

If the ball is impacted anywhere but in the center of the clubhead, it will cause rotation during impact. The cluhead rotates one way and the ball the opposite.

IMPACT POSITION AFFECTS SPIN, SMASH-FACTOR AND CURVE.

heel strike

LAUNCH ANGLE

Identifying your launch angle is an essential step to increasing your distance off the tee. Launch angle looks at clubhead and ball speed, spin, carry, and landing angle using technology such as TrackMan.

POWER TECHNIQUE

What is your LAUNCH ANGLE?

Driver

6-Iron

TOUR AVERAGES

PGA TOUR

Driver – 10.9 degrees

6 iron – 14.1 degrees

LPGA TOUR

Driver – 13.2 degrees

6 iron – 17.1 degrees

MALE AMATEUR (DRIVER)

Scratch of Better – 11.2 degrees

5 HCP – 11.2 degrees

10 HCP – 11.9 degrees

Average Golfer (14.5) – 12.6 degrees

Bogey Golfer – 12.1 degrees

FEMALE AMATEUR (DRIVER)

Scratch or Better – 12.7 degrees

5 HCP – 12.0 degrees

10 HCP – 12.4 degrees

15 HCP – 13.6 degrees

TRACKMAN

DYNAMIC LOFT **+** ATTACK ANGLE = LAUNCH ANGLE

Launch Angle represents the vertical angle at which the ball leaves a player's clubface after being struck. It is the angle the ball takes off at relative to the horizon. Along with ball speed, it is the primary component to determining and optimizing the height and distance of a shot.

OPTIMIZE LAUNCH ANGLE

as defined by TrackMan

LAUNCH ANGLE

The vertical angle relative to the horizon of the golf ball's center of gravity movement immediately after leaving the club face.

EXAMPLES OF
OPTIMAL LAUNCH ANGLE BASED ON
CLUBHEAD SPEED, ASSUMING
0° ATTACK ANGLE

14°
12°   16°
10°   20°
<75
CLUBHEAD SPEED

88

14°

12°

16°

10°

20°

85
CLUBHEAD SPEED

14°
12°
16°
10°
20°

95-100
CLUBHEAD SPEED

KEY POINT

Driver Optimizer Chart at
the end of this section.

SPIN RATE IS THE RATE OF ROTATION JUST AFTER IMPACT

92

SPIN RATE

Spin rate (backspin, not forward spin) has a major influence on the height and distance of a shot. Spin is created through your clubhead speed and spin loft (direction clubhead is moving and the face orientation at the point of impact).

DYNAMIC LOFT - ATTACK ANGLE = SPIN RATE

as defined by TrackMan

SPIN RATE - The rate of rotation of the golf ball around the resulting rotational axis of the golf ball immediately after the golf ball separates from the clubface.

FACTORS THAT AFFECT SPIN

Spin Loft
Clubhead Speed
Impact Position
Club Design
Ball Design
Friction

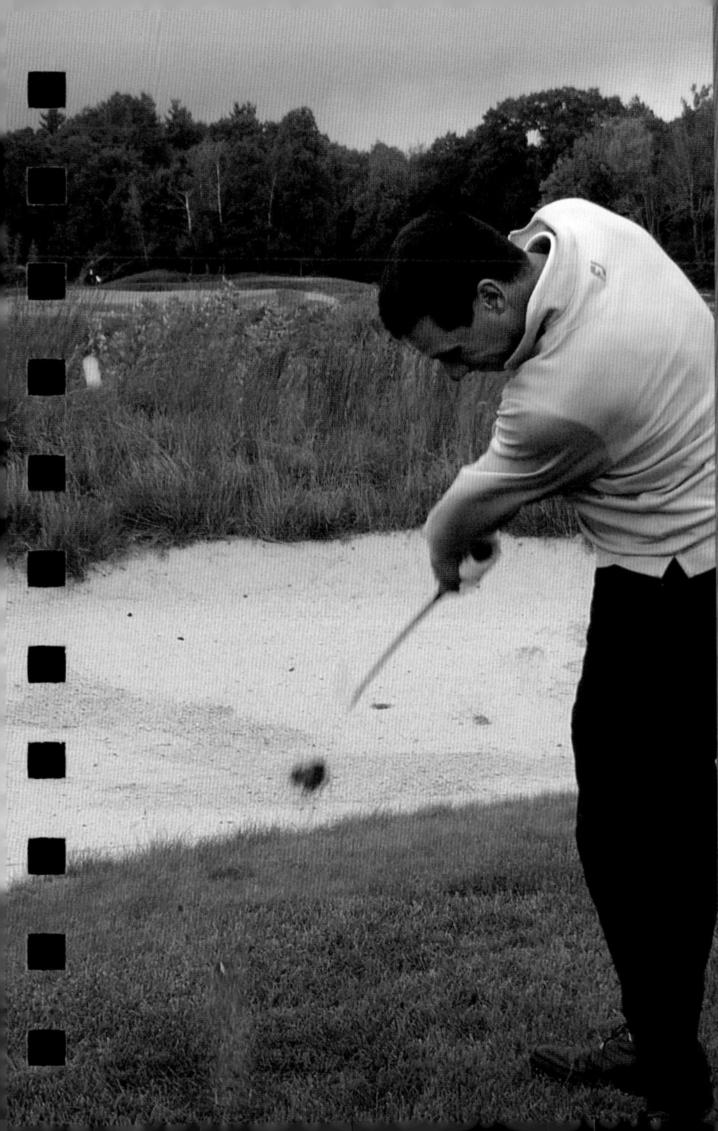

SPIN LOFT & RATE

Spin Loft is the difference between Dynamic Loft (face orientation at the point of impact) and Attack Angle (direction club is moving). Along with clubhead speed, spin loft is one of the major influencers of your overall Spin Rate.

POWER TECHNIQUE

What is your SPIN RATE?

Driver

6-Iron

{ TRACKMAN STATS SPIN RATE & SPIN LOFT }

PGA TOUR

Driver – 2686 rpm

Driver - 14.7 degrees

6 iron – 6231 rpm

6-iron - 24.3 degrees

LPGA TOUR

Driver – 2611 rpm

Driver - 15.0 degrees

6 iron – 5943 rpm

6-iron - 25.9 degrees

MALE AMATEUR (DRIVER)

Scratch – 2896 rpm/14.8 degrees

5 HCP – 2987 rpm/15.8

10 HCP – 3192 rpm/17.3

Avg Golfer – 3275 rpm/18.3

Bogey Golfer – 3127 rpm/18.2

FEMALE AMATEUR (DRIVER)

Scratch – 2831 rpm/17.1 degrees

5 HCP – 3027 rpm/18.4

10 HCP – 3207 rpm/18.6

15 HCP – 3287 rpm/20.1

TRACKMAN

BALL SPEED

BALL SPEED HAS THE
GREATEST INFLUENCE ON DISTANCE.

Hooks, slices or hitting too down on the ball can also reduce ball speed. Although club speed is key to distance, the ball speed that is created at impact is the biggest factor in how far the ball actually carries.

GAINING 1 MPH OF BALL SPEED CAN INCREASE YOUR DRIVER DISTANCE BY UP TO 2 YARDS.

as defined by TrackMan

BALL SPEED – The speed of the golf ball's center of gravity immediately after separation from the clubface.

BALL SPEED

Ball Speed is the speed of the golf ball immediately after impact. Ball speed is created by club speed and impact. Poor impact, such as shots hit on the toe or heel, will reduce the ball speed.

POWER TECHNIQUE

What is your BALL SPEED?

Driver

6-Iron

TOUR AVERAGES

PGA TOUR
Driver – 168 mph

LPGA TOUR
Driver – 140mph

> ## TRACKMAN STATS
> ### BALL SPEED

MALE AMATEUR (DRIVER)
Scratch of Better – 161 mph
5 HCP – 147 mph
10 HCP – 138 mph
Average Golfer (14.5) – 133 mph
Bogey Golfer – 131 mph

FEMALE AMATEUR (DRIVER)
Scratch or Better – 131 mph
5 HCP – 125 mph
10 HCP – 119 mph
15 HCP – 111 mph

TRACKMAN

SMASH-FACTOR

Smash-factor relates to the amount of energy transferred from the club head to the golf ball.

The higher the smash-factor, the better the energy transfer. A golfer would hope to achieve a smash-factor near 1.50 on driver shots.

The higher the loft of the club, the lower the smash-factor is expected to be. A PW should have a smash-factor near 1.25.

SMASH-FACTOR IS BALL SPEED DIVIDED BY CLUB SPEED

Smash-factor influence on distance is significant. For example, Bill has a club speed of 100 mph and a smash-factor of 1.40. Bill's ball speed is 140 mph. His buddy Sam has a club speed of 100 mph and a smash-factor of 1.50. Sam's ball speed is 150 mph. The **10 mph difference in ball speed** between Bill and Sam, equates to approximately **20 yards in distance**, even though they have the same club speed. Hitting center-face optimizes smash-factor.

SMASH-FACTOR

Smash-factor relates to the amount of energy transferred from the club head to the golf ball. Focus on center face strikes to optimize this number.

POWER TECHNIQUE

What is your smash-factor?

Driver

6-Iron

TOUR AVERAGES

PGA TOUR

Driver – 1.49
6 iron – 1.38

LPGA TOUR

Driver – 1.49
6 iron – 1.39

TRACKMAN STATS SMASH-FACTOR

MALE AMATEUR (DRIVER)

Scratch of Better – 1.49
5 HCP – 1.45
10 HCP – 1.45
Average Golfer (14.5) – 1.44
Bogey Golfer – 1.43

FEMALE AMATEUR (DRIVER)

Scratch or Better – 1.46
5 HCP – 1.45
10 HCP – 1.44
15 HCP – 1.41

TRACKMAN

IMPACT POINT

FORGED FACE

LAUNCHES HIGHER
LESS SPIN

DRAW FLIGHT
LESS SPIN

SLICE FLIGHT
MORE SPIN

LAUNCHES LOWER
MORE SPIN

GET CENTER CONTACT FOR OPTIMAL
SMASH-FACTOR, SPIN AND BALL SPEED.
Higher on the face creates less spin, and
lower on the face creates more spin.

Optimize your impact point, clubhead speed and attack angle. Optimizing these will produce an optimal ball speed, launch angle and spin rate.

IMPACT POINT

Where are your IMPACT POSITIONS?

TAKE ACTION

Mark with a marker or place your impact stickers on the faces.

DRIVER OPTIMIZER CHART

CLUBHEAD SPEED (mph)	ATTACK ANGLE (deg)	BALL SPEED (mph)	LAUNCH ANGLE (deg)
75	-5	107	11.8
	0	109	13.0
	5	111	15.3
80	-5	115	10.1
	0	117	12.1
	5	118	14.8
85	-5	123	9.3
	0	125	11.7
	5	126	14.0
90	-5	131	8.5
	0	132	10.8
	5	134	13.8
95	-5	138	7.9
	0	140	10.5
	5	141	13.0

SPIN RATE (rpm)	CARRY (yards)	TOTAL (yards)	DYNAMIC LOFT (deg)
3214	140	182	14.9
2506	147	195	15.3
1976	156	206	17.1
3078	154	188	12.8
2494	163	199	14.3
2005	174	209	16.5
3110	169	215	11.9
2568	180	228	13.8
1964	189	241	15.6
3122	185	231	11.0
2517	196	245	12.8
2021	207	259	15.3
3144	201	247	10.2
2565	213	262	12.3
1948	223	276	14.4

BALL FLIGHT
GET WHAT YOU WANT

What is your desired ball flight? Do you currently have it? If not, let's find out why. After reading this section, as well as the Ball Flight Laws section, you'll be well-educated on the whys. By understanding the whys, you can create real change.

Let's begin with start direction. Balls either start left, on, or right of the target. Pretty simple. The key is to determine whether this start direction is providing your desired ball flight and distance. If not, let's determine if it's a face issue, path issue or a bit of both.

DESIRED BALL FLIGHT OVERVIEW

If you do not have access to a TrackMan or similar device, set up a ball flight assessment station as shown. Use a pool noodle, bright construction ribbon and some tees. Hit 10 balls with your 7-iron, and 10 more with your driver. Have a pal film or watch. However, with this set up, you should be able to see, as well.

BALL FLIGHT
ASSESSMENT

Where's your ball starting? Are you
sure? Let's find out...*for sure.*

Once we determine your current stats, then we can begin a plan to create real change.

TAKE ACTION

Head to the MorePars.com platform to enter and track your stats.

116

BALL FLIGHT
LET'S STATE YOURS NOW

Desired Ball Flight Driver:

My Driver Shots Start:

Ball Curves Typically:

Desired Ball Flight Irons:

My Iron Shots Start:

Ball Curves:

Carry Distance with Driver:

Carry Distance with 7-Iron:

Equipment is Fitted:

Current Swing Characteristics:

HOW TO

CHANGE YOUR BALL FLIGHT

When it comes to modifying your ball flight—which includes where it starts, how it curves and how far it travels—we need to first assess. What is your face angle at the point of impact, and the club's path, both in relation to the target line? **Face angle has more influence than club path on the start direction.** The ball will always start in a direction that is between your club path and face angle. **Where you strike on the face** also plays a big role in your start direction, especially with a driver, as it has a curved face, referred to as bulge.

WITH A DRIVER, FACE ANGLE INFLUENCES
85% & CLUB PATH ONLY 15%.

EQUIPMENT CONSIDERATIONS

Your equipment also plays a vital role. It's important to ensure that these variables are optimized for your game:

- Grip Size
- Shaft Length
- Shaft Flex
- Head Design

- Lie Angle
- Weight
- Loft
- COG Placement

POWER EQUIPMENT

LIE ANGLE
MEASURING
DEVICE

Each manufacturer has a different spec for the lie angle on their clubs. Lie angle is one of the most important fitting variables to get right when you buy a set of irons. A majority of golfers never consider lie angle when purchasing irons. For example, a lie angle that is too flat will tend to open the face through impact. Too upright will tend to close the face (club is steeper) and start the ball left. Shaft length can affect impact point, as well.

FACE TO PATH

More often than not, the set up is the primary dictator of what will occur in-motion (next section). In-motion components that affect launch direction and curvature include:

- Swing Direction relative to the target line
- Attack Angle • Face Angle • Clubhead Path

These elements together affect the launch direction (start) and spin axis (curvature).

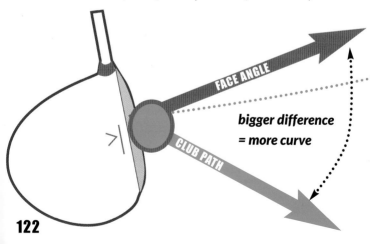

FACE ANGLE

bigger difference = more curve

CLUB PATH

A positive face to path means the face is pointed to the right of the club path, regardless of dexterity.

A negative face to path means the face is pointed to the left of the club path.

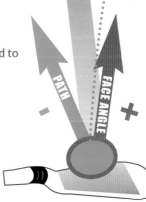

KEY POINT

SLICES & HOOKS

If the face of the club is closed relative to the path the clubhead is traveling at the moment of the strike, the ball will tend to hook. If the face is open to the path, the ball will slice. *The bigger the difference between the face and the path, the more the ball will curve.*

123

STEEP OR SHALLOW
WHAT ARE YOU?

Understanding steeps and shallows will make your improvement process much easier. A steeper angle of attack tends to produce an out-to-in path with more spin, where a shallow path tends to move the path more in-to-out and less spin. A shallow path will tend to create a more open face angle at impact, where a steeper angle will tend to close the face.

A fade ball flight (steep) is an out-to-in path (more spin, less roll once it lands). A draw ball flight produces an in-to-out path (shallow with less spin and more roll-out).

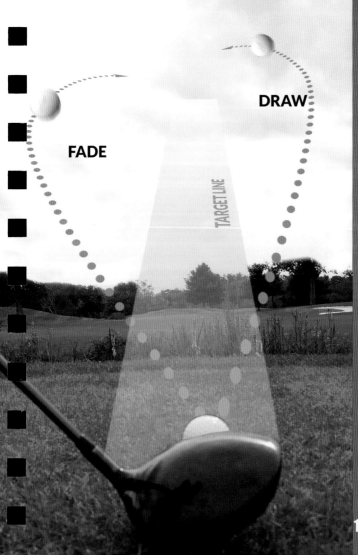

FADE

DRAW

TARGET LINE

SET UP A STEEP & SHALLOW PLANE STATION to determine your current swing plane. Set the noodle so it is at or just above your driver's shaft at address and runs through your trail elbow, as shown.

A fade, straight or draw ball flight are considered playable ball flights as they end up at the target. Fades won't travel as far as a draw ball flight.

STRAIGHT SHOT

SHALLOW DELIVERY

Your shallow if the club
travels under the noodle
and does not make
contact with the noodle.

STEEP DELIVERY

If you make contact with the noodle,
your downswing is steep.

IF YOU'RE TOO STEEP:

PULLS AND SLICES

FAT SHOTS

DEEP DIVOTS

TOE HITS

IF YOU'RE TOO SHALLOW:

PUSHES AND HOOKS

THIN SHOTS

NO DIVOTS

HEEL HITS

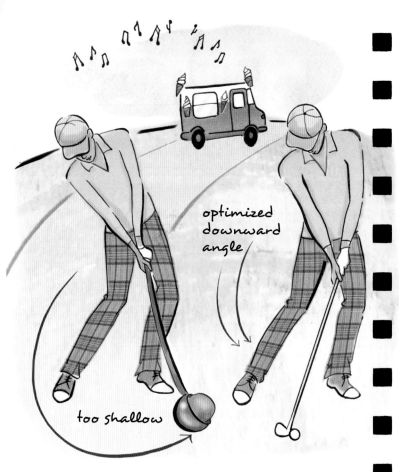

optimized
downward
angle

too shallow

A more shallow approach will tend to swing
up on the ball, whereas a steeper descent will
strike down with too much attack angle.

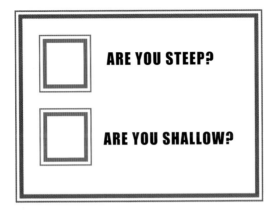

ARE YOU STEEP?

ARE YOU SHALLOW?

Knowing whether you are steep or shallow also plays a key role in shots from the fairway (as do your swing characteristic tendencies). In fact, these are at the core of how the ball comes off the face, from your address to in-motion. Your set-up should be your first step to get your desired ball flight. Now that you have determined whether you're steep or shallow, this should align with your current ball flight.

SET-UP
YOUR FIRST STEP

In this next section, we'll cover in detail what to look for in your SET-UP and how modifications can alter your start direction. Your SET-UP is the first step to creating a change. In fact, small changes in your address positions can have significant gains.

SET-UP INCLUDES:

- Grip
- Ball Position
- Torso Bend
- Stance Width
- Alignment
- Head Position
- Weight Distribution
- Shaft Position

TAKE ACTION

Head to MorePars.com to view this section!

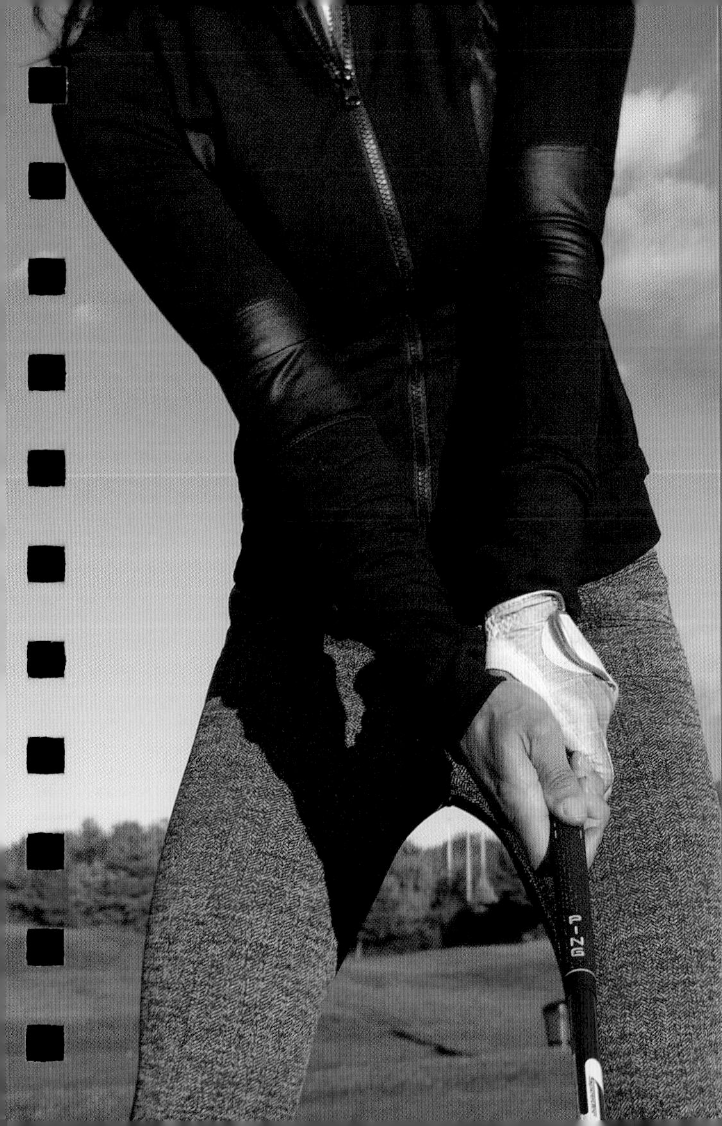
PING

SWING CHARACTERISTICS
EFFECT ON FACE AND PATH

Swing characteristics can affect club path, attack angle and face angle. Understanding your swing tendencies and how that may influence your current ball flight is the first step to optimizing face and path.

TAKE ACTION

Head to MorePars.com to view this section!

face

path

POSTURE

REVERSE SPINE

POWER LEAKS

SWING CHARACTERISTICS & FIXES

There are a collection of common Swing Characteristics that rob power and efficiency. The first step is to identify yours. The second step is to identify a solution.

OVER THE TOP

SHOULDER PLANE

SWAY & SLIDES

CASTING

EARLY EXTENSION

CHICKEN WING

HANG BACK

THE NATURAL
CURVE OF
YOUR SPINE

FIND
NEUTRAL

POSTURE
LEAKS

It all begins at address with your POSTURE. Establishing good posture that can support your golf swing is paramount. To create distance and consistency, maintaining this posture thoughout the swing is also critical. To keep our spine safe, swing in neutral.

POSSIBLE CULPRITS

- **Muscle imbalances**
- **Equipment**
- **Lack of awareness**
- **Inability to pelvic tilt**
- **Inability to hip hinge**
- **Too much knee flex**

C-POSTURE

POSSIBLE CULPRITS OF C-POSTURE

- Muscle imbalances: limited thoracic spine extension, tight chest, neck flexors or weak core
- Equipment considerations - Length of clubs
- Inability to pelvic tilt and/or hip hinge
- Too much knee flex
- Lack of awareness

Excessive roundness (pelvic posterior tilt) will not support a rotational backswing. Players will most likely rise up and out of their posture.

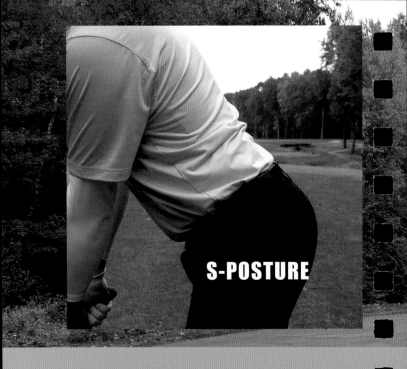

S-POSTURE

POSSIBLE CULPRITS OF S-POSTURE

- Muscle imbalances: Tight hip flexors, weak glutes and abdominals
- Lack of awareness
- Inability to pelvic tuck and/or hip hinge
- Too much knee flex

Excessive arch (anterior pelvic tilt) will not support a power backswing. Players will most likely rise up during the backswing and early extend on the downswing.

NEUTRAL

A neutral spine keeps our spine safe and our golf swing powered up. It engages the midline and ensures that our lower back (lumbar) is not compromised.

KEY POINT

The key is to hinge from your hip sockets with a soft back and engaged core.

149

ON THE COURSE

Incorporate squeezing an orange during your pre-shot routine.

FIND A WALL AND MAKE ANGELS. Stand (which is easier) or take a seat, which strengthens your legs at the same time.

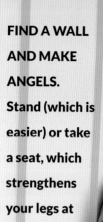

DON'T DO THIS

Don't arch the back at any point.

STEP 1

HOME OR GYM

Slowly raise and
lower your arms,
while keeping your
back against the wall.

STEP 2

153

BACKSWING
LEAKS

Maintaining your posture throughout the backswing is paramount for an efficient golf swing. Backswing LOSS OF POSTURE is a popular leak and can affect timing, balance, rhythm and centerface contact. Other backswing leaks could be a lack of weight transfer, limited arm height or not fully rotating the back, due to thoracic limitations.

POSSIBLE CULPRITS

- Scapula instability, weak core or glutes, tightness in thoracic, lats, shoulders, hips, neck, hamstrings or limited ankle mobility
- Lack of awareness
- Inability to perform a deep squat or hip hinge
- Inability to separate upper from lower body

Loss of posture is
for the birds.

FLAT
SHOULDER PLANE

TAKE ACTION

Flat Shoulder Plane can be diagnosed by a pal, coach or camera. A player with the Flat Shoulder characteristic will have a more vertical spine angle with the shoulders more horizontal to the ground. It may also take the club out of position at the top of the backswing or affect the downswing plane. Things to test: Pelvic Tilt, Glutes, Seated Trunk, Lats, Ankles, Lower Quarter Rotation.

< 30°

Loss of posture during
the backswing causes
the body and/or hands
to compensate on the
downswing to square
the club face. This can
also cause a loss of
power in the swing, as
well as inconsistent ball
striking.

IDEAL
SHOULDER PLANE

In an ideal world, the shoulders should move perpendicular to the tilt of the spine on the backswing. You'll feel your lead shoulder point towards the ground.

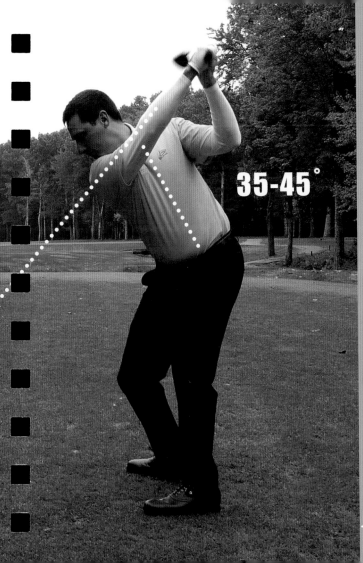

35-45°

REVERSE
SPINE

REVERSE SPINE ANGLE is characterized by an excessive torso lean towards the target during the backswing. This swing fault makes it a challenge to sequence the downswing. Oftentimes, the upper body overpowers the downswing, resulting in an over-the-top move.

POSSIBLE CULPRITS

- S-Posture
- Limited internal hip rotation (tight back hip)
- Limited ability to separate upper and lower
- Lateral Sway during backswing
- Trying to keep your eye on the ball (stay centered)
- Poor head position at address

KEY POINT

Reverse spine is a dangerous position for your lower back, as well. It compresses lumbar discs in your effort to get back into position during the downswing.

161

NO

Spine angled
toward target
with loss of knee
flex in trail leg.

162

YES

Spine angled away from target with knee flex in trail leg.

DO THIS If your trail hip is not limited, sit into your back hip so it goes back toward the target.

NO

HEAD POSITION

Poor head position at address can result in reverse spine angle. If you tilt your head excessively toward the target at address, your backswing will follow suit.

YES

Chin in line
with your
spine at
address.

NO

VISUALIZE A WHITE PICKET FENCE.
For those that sway, your trail hip would make contact with the fence, but your spine would be angled away.

YES

Get your chest over the fence with your trail hip moving away from the fence.

NO

- Lateral move, where pressure points favor the outside of trail leg
- The trail hip shifts excessively away from target
- Knee not stabilizing, points excessively away from target
- Foot not stabilizing, rolls outward

YES

- Sit into the trail hip
- Pressure favors the inside of the trail leg

POSSIBLE CULPRITS SWAYERS

- C-Posture
- Knee or Ankle immobility - inability to evert
- Limited internal hip rotation (tight back hip)
- Limited ability to separate upper and lower
- Limited glute strength

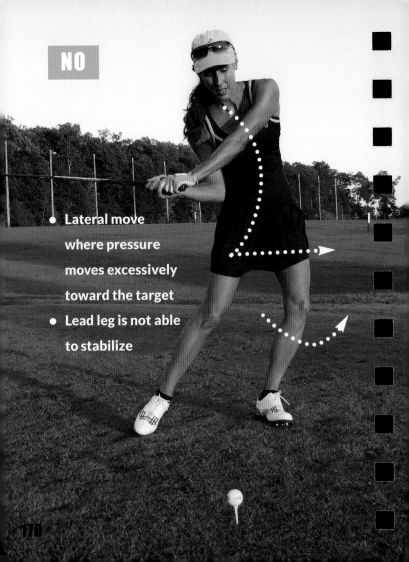

NO

- Lateral move where pressure moves excessively toward the target
- Lead leg is not able to stabilize

170

YES

- Lead leg stable as the lead hip moves upward and away from target

POSSIBLE CULPRITS SLIDERS

- Ankle immobility - inability to invert or evert
- Lead hip internal rotation
- Trail leg external rotation
- Inability to separate lower from upper body
- Lack of glute strength in lead leg

171

DO THIS

Push out like
riding a horse to
activate the legs

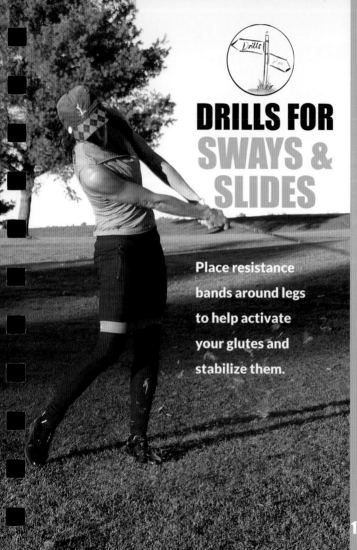

DRILLS FOR
SWAYS & SLIDES

Place resistance bands around legs to help activate your glutes and stabilize them.

BAND ON LEAD FOR SWAYERS

Wrap heavy tubing
around your pal's
lead hip.

Nick is a lefty. Christina wraps the band on his hip, then pulls toward her, which forces Nick to work extra hard to stabilize that trail side.

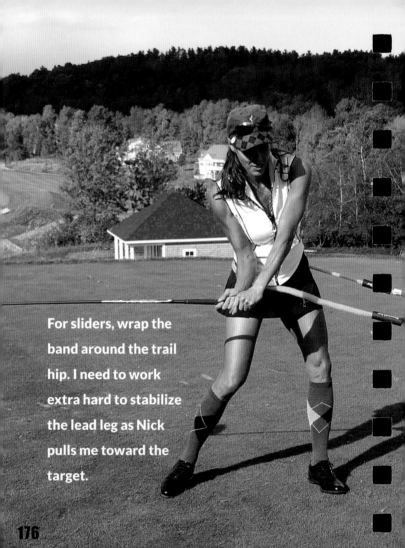

For sliders, wrap the band around the trail hip. I need to work extra hard to stabilize the lead leg as Nick pulls me toward the target.

SINGLE LEG
SWINGS
SWAY

FOR SWAYERS,
stand on the trail leg
and make swings. If
you move too much
laterally, you'll fall
off balance.

SINGLE LEG
SWINGS
SLIDE

FOR SLIDERS,
stand on lead leg and
make swings. If you
move excessively
toward the target,
you'll fall off balance.

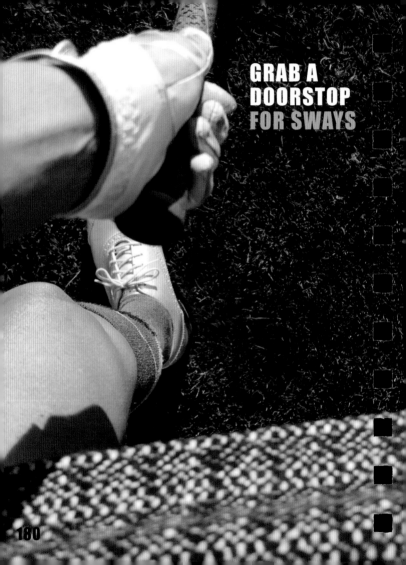

GRAB A
DOORSTOP
FOR SWAYS

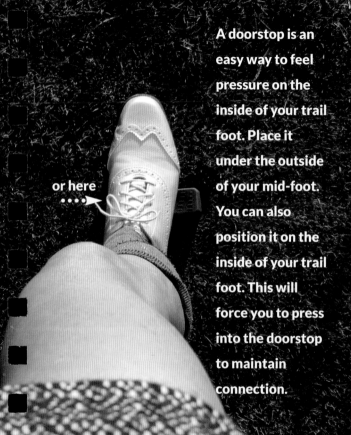

or here

A doorstop is an easy way to feel pressure on the inside of your trail foot. Place it under the outside of your mid-foot. You can also position it on the inside of your trail foot. This will force you to press into the doorstop to maintain connection.

GO WIDE

WITH YOUR STANCE

If your tendency is to sway or slide, try a wider stance. **A wider stance stabilizes your legs, making it a challenge to sway or slide.**

However, a wider stance will also make it a bit more challenging to get to a full finish. Experiment with width-of-stance to see what works best for your swing.

OVER THE TOP

NO

HANDS AND SHAFT ARE ABOVE THE PLANE.
To view an over the-top move, view from behind (down the line view) the target line.

DOWNSWING
LEAKS

OVER THE TOP is a common swing fault among players. The upper body initiates the downswing over the lower body, resulting in a throwing action out towards the ball (referred to as outside to in). An over-the-top move results in a pull, if the clubface is square or closed, or a slice if the club face is open.

POSSIBLE CULPRITS

- Ankle mobility - inability to invert or evert
- Lead hip internal rotation
- Trail leg external rotation
- Inability to separate lower and upper body
- Glute and core strength

Too many swing
thoughts can
wreak havoc on
the downswing.

YES

The shaft is behind my body, not out toward ball.

Leading the downswing with the lower body DROPS the hands/club down into the delivery slot for an inside path.

DRILLS FOR OVER THE TOP

FIND A WALL.
Position yourself
10-12 inches in
front of the wall.
Slowly, take the
club back until it
touches the wall.

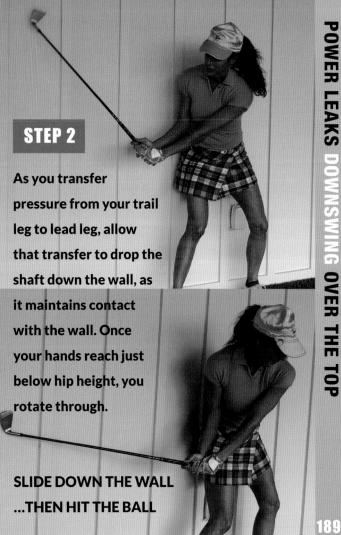

STEP 2

As you transfer pressure from your trail leg to lead leg, allow that transfer to drop the shaft down the wall, as it maintains contact with the wall. Once your hands reach just below hip height, you rotate through.

SLIDE DOWN THE WALL ...THEN HIT THE BALL

189

YES

CREATE A TARGET MARK ON YOUR BALL.
Position it on the inside path. Use that as a
visual to strike, as you move through impact.
It's a great training visual to promote an inside
path without over-thinking the mechanics.

STRIKE THE
INSIDE OF
THE BALL

NO

If you strike the outside of the ball, you know that you are still coming over-the-top with an out to inside path.

Place a shaft
through your
belt line.

TRAIN
DISASSOCIATION

192

Use it as a visual guide as you stabilize the upper body with your driver shaft. This is also a great pre-round stretch.

NO

Hands moving out
towards the ball,
throws the club on
an overly outward
approach.

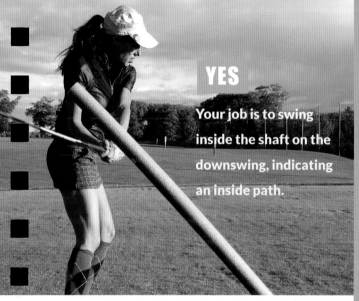

YES

Your job is to swing inside the shaft on the downswing, indicating an inside path.

NOODLE DRILL

With any swing path change, it is important to feel the complete opposite of what you are currently doing. If it feels the same, you are probably not doing it. Training aids that provide visual or kinesthetic feedback are the fastest path to more pars. Pun intended :-)

STEP & GO FOR LEG DRIVE

STEP 1

As you turn into your backswing, lift your lead leg off the ground.

STEP 2

Step with that same foot into the ground

with force to train lower body initiation.

NO

Body moves
up and
toward ball.

198

EARLY
EXTENSION

EARLY EXTENSION is forward movement (thrust) of the lower body toward the golf ball during the downswing. This crowds the ball and forces a player to eject out of their posture. Early Extension typically results in a block to the right or a hook to the left.

POSSIBLE CULPRITS

- C-Posture and pelvic tuck/tilt control
- Ankle mobility - inability to invert or evert
- Inability to hip hinge, such as deep squat
- Glute and core weakness
- Inability to disassociate lower from upper
- Lead hip or knee restrictions
- Misconception of how to swing in to out

199

YES

Hips clear away
from the ball to
make room for
the club.

200

The lower body clears the way on the downswing by moving away from the ball. This requires good external lead hip mobility, plus core and glute strength to stabilize this movement.

SINGLE ARM SWINGS

STEP 1

Single arm swings, either with your lead or trail arm, help to create a rotation away from the ball. Focus on clearing your lead hip away from the ball on the downswing.

STEP 2

STEP 1

As you turn into your backswing, your back cheek stays in contact with the chair.

GRAB A CHAIR

STEP 2

As you turn into your downswing, your lead cheek stays in contact with the chair.

A great way to train at home or in the office.

NO

KEEP YOUR CHEST FACING DOWN

YES

Early extenders rise up and out of their posture. A great mental visual is to keep your chest facing down to the ground, back and through your swing.

angles gone

EARLY RELEASE CASTING

On their quest to get more lag, players fall off the downswing track

POSSIBLE CULPRITS

- Wrist or forearm limitations - trail and lead

- Sequence issues - upper body dominant

- Sways and Slides

- Inability to separate lower and upper body

- Lead ankle, knee or hip limitations

- Misconception of how to maintain angles

NO

A lost connection with your last
three fingers may cause the
club to feel heavy and fall away.

If your pinkie, ring and middle fingers lose a firm
connection to the grip, the club will fall away. This
is one of the important reasons we wear a glove!

YES

These three fingers are the key to leveraging the weight of the club.

Your pinkie, ring and middle fingers are the drivers during the backswing, ensuring backswing extension and leverage of the club.

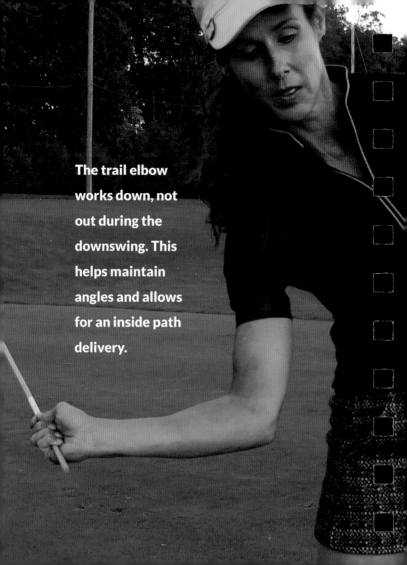

The trail elbow works down, not out during the downswing. This helps maintain angles and allows for an inside path delivery.

ELBOW LEADS THE WAY

STEP 1

Feel like gravity is dropping the club down, initiated by a weight transfer to your lead side. Transfer of pressure is what drops the club and maintains angles.

CHEST IS **PASSIVE,** AS THE ARM SLIDES DOWN.

80% weight here

STEP 2

215

The term Chicken Wing in golf refers to a bent lead arm post-impact.

216

NO

A bent lead arm and cupped wrist keep the face open through impact, creating too much spin.

POST-IMPACT LEAKS

POSSIBLE CULPRITS

- Sequence issues - upper body dominant
- Lack of lead shoulder external rotation
- Wrist or forearm limitations
- Steep downswing path
- Misconceptions about how to release

RELEASE
THE CLUB

The wrists and forearms are a major power source, providing lots of clubhead speed. The trail hand is on top allowing the club to close, which creates great extension through the shot.

YES

NO

ELIMINATE THE
CHICKEN WING
by placing a head
cover under the
lead arm. This will
help to promote a
forearm rotation
with a better
release.

YES

DRILLS
TO
ELIMINATE

ZIP-ZIP
FOR BETTER CONNECTION

If you struggle with the release or a disconnection
with your arms to your torso during the backswing
or downswing, visualize zippers. Mentally, zipping
up your upper arms to your torso helps to keep
your swing's structure, back and through.

Zip-zip to promote more torso-to-arm engagement.

To keep the chickens in the barn!

TRAIL HAND
ON TOP

NO

TRAIL HAND UNDERNEATH
This can promote an upward
strike, which is not what we want
for fairway shots. Closing the face
from this position is extra work
and oftentimes results in the
chicken wing.

YES

TRAIL HAND ON TOP
This creates a
powerful position to
strike down and
through.

BALL FOR CONNECTION

Place a ball between your arms. This is a dog toy turned into a fun training aid to help maintain connection, back and through.

228

BUNGEE FOR CONNECTION

A bungee cord is an inexpensive way to feel connection in your golf swing. It needs to be snug to work.

RELEASE
CONCEPTION

NO

Many players are not crystal clear on how to release the club. Grab a magnetic pointer to provide a visual of where your clubface is as you do slow-motion swings. If your pointer points skyward, you did not release.

YES

Magnetic
pointer should
be parallel to
the ground at
this point past
impact.

DON'T DO THIS

Don't
actually
swing, as the
pointer will
go flying
away.

80%

20%

232

POST-IMPACT
HANG BACK

The HANG BACK refers to keeping too much weight on the trail side during the downswing, and into the finish. Weight transfer is a major player in the golf swing. When this is compromised, so is clubhead speed and contact.

POSSIBLE CULPRITS

- Lack of lead ankle mobility
- Lack of hip mobility or stability
- Lower body weakness, limiting transfer ability
- Lead knee issues
- Reverse spine or pivot
- Too much side bend at address

EXCESSIVE
SIDE BEND

NO

With an excessive
side bend, you'll
promote hitting up on
the ball. This will most
likely result in a thin
or fat shot.

YES

GET STACKED with your torso over the ball promoting the lead hip to stack over the knee and ankle for max leverage, stability and power.

235

LET A SHAFT BE
YOUR GUIDE

Use a shaft to groove a complete finish,
where your body lines are facing left of the
target for right-handed players and right for
left-handed players.

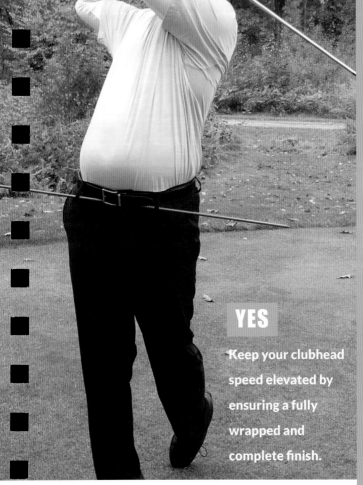

YES

Keep your clubhead speed elevated by ensuring a fully wrapped and complete finish.

STEP FOR TRANSFER

A great way to feel a true weight transfer is to lift your lead heel or entire foot during the backswing...then plant it firmly **to initiate your downswing.**

STEP 1

STEP 2

WRAP YOUR
SHOULDER

Transfer your weight by fully wrapping your trail shoulder all the way through, so that it is left of the target (for right-handed player).

MORE DISTANCE
GET THE DISTANCE YOU WANT

This section covers key points to guide you to your efficient swing. Efficiency gives us consistency and the best chance for center-face contact. In fact, if you just focus on achieving center-face, you'll experience significant gains off the tee and from the fairway. Nick and Christina share their swings with keys to help you with yours! There is no cookie-cutter swing, but there are some essential keys to optimize center-face and efficiency. From there, we'll dive into Power Modifications. We'll borrow power secrets from the longest ball strikers on the planet. Yes, the World Long Drive Champs that kill it over 400 yards, breaking all the rules along the way...and the speed barrier. Let's adopt some of their power secrets.

So, let's get to it!

MAXIMIZE
BALL SPEED

OPTIMIZE YOUR
- **SPIN**
- **LAUNCH ANGLE**
- **IMPACT POINT**

These shots will have a higher smash-factor.

These shots will have a lower smash-factor.

CENTER-FACE

When it comes to generating distance, the golden rule is center-face contact.

TAKE ACTION

Where on the face are you making contact? Apply foot powder or impact stickers to find out. Anything but center will affect ball speed, spin, curvature, and distance.

DRIVER
KEY POINTS

- Neutral spine
- Weight pressure balls of feet
- Shoulders in line with toes
- Shaft of driver pointing to belt line

246

- Chin in line with sternum
- Sternum in line with the edge of the driver to optimize launch
- Ball off lead heel
- Feet flared to promote easy back and through swing
- More weight favoring trail leg

45%

55%

TAKEAWAY
& PRESSURE TRANSFER

- **Shoulder pointing down maintaining posture**
- **Hands close to body maintaining a connected takeaway**

80%

- Chest driving a wide takeaway
- 80% of weight on trail leg when lead arm parallel
- Pressure points favoring inside of trail leg

249

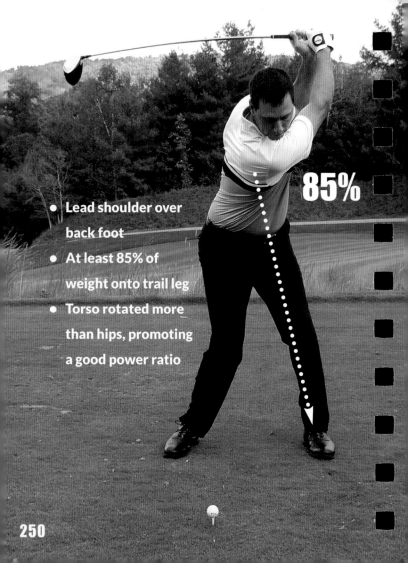

85%

- Lead shoulder over back foot
- At least 85% of weight onto trail leg
- Torso rotated more than hips, promoting a good power ratio

250

BACKSWING
LOAD UP

- Spine and belt angles keep posture intact
- Arms in front of chest (not too deep behind body)

75%

- Pressure already back to lead side
- Shoulders passive as legs drive pressure to lead side

TRANSITION
PRESSURE MOVES TO FRONT

- Hands and club track down (not out) during this pressure transfer to lead side
- Hinge increases as he transitions

85%

● Knees and hips parallel to target line as torso is yet to unwind, allowing the hands to drop into the power slot

254

SEQUENCE
DURING DOWNSWING

- Hips clearing away from ball and upward to make room for club
- Chest is still square, keeping the club on plane
- Hands close to thighs
- Good footwork with trail heel off the ground indicating good pressure transfer to lead side

80°
HEAD
ANGLE

● Head
quiet, to
allow the
club and
hands to
pass

● Getting
vertical as
he moves
through
impact for a
burst of
explosive
power

Angles intact

- Path is inside
- Angle in trail wrist intact
- Hips still clearing

257

80°
HEAD

- Head still at 80 degrees, hasn't budged
- Trail hand crosses over lead, indicating good release with wrists
- Almost airborne from the vertical thrust

258

VERTICAL
JUMP FOR EXPLOSIVE POWER

- Good wrist and forearm release
- A vertical thrust producing great force
- Trail foot on toes

259

- **Head still at 80 degrees, hasn't budged well past impact**
- **Trail hand still crossing over as forearms fully rotated**

260

CLUB EXITS
ON PLANE

- Club exiting on lead shoulder, indicating good attack angle
- Still in his posture as indicated by his lead shoulder down and torso side bend

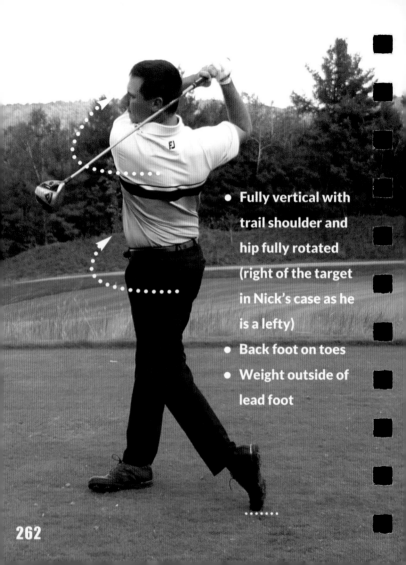

- **Fully vertical with trail shoulder and hip fully rotated (right of the target in Nick's case as he is a lefty)**
- **Back foot on toes**
- **Weight outside of lead foot**

- All spikes and body lines right of the target, indicating complete finish, which keeps the clubhead speed elevated

263

SWING TEMPO

THE GLUE THAT PUTS IT ALL TOGETHER

3

Backswing Time .75

An ideal ratio for backswing time and downswing-to-impact time is 3 to 1 with a driver. The backswing takes 3 times as long as the downswing.

1

Downswing Time .25

IRON
KEY
POINTS

- Neutral spine
- Shoulders in line with toes
- Shaft of iron pointing to belt line

- Sternum in line with the ball
- Feet flared to promote unrestricted rotation, back and through
- Weight pressure balls of feet

55%

45%

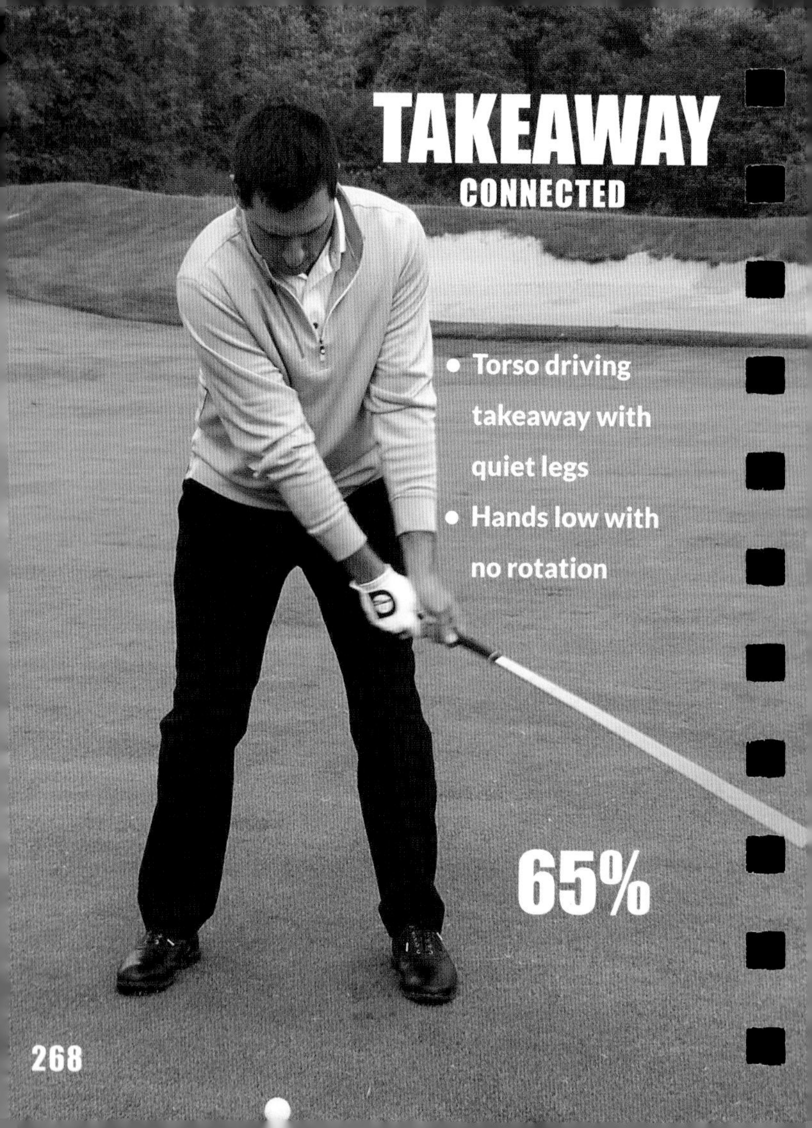

TAKEAWAY
CONNECTED

- Torso driving takeaway with quiet legs
- Hands low with no rotation

65%

268

- **Nick is taking the club back square as indicated by his trail hand on top and the clubface mirroring his spine angle**

- **Hands tracking over toes indicating a connected takeaway**

- **Hands still low with no rotation**
- **Hips beginning to rotate in reaction to upper body**

75%

270

- Shoulder plane down indicating good posture

- Legs remain very quiet at this point in the swing

271

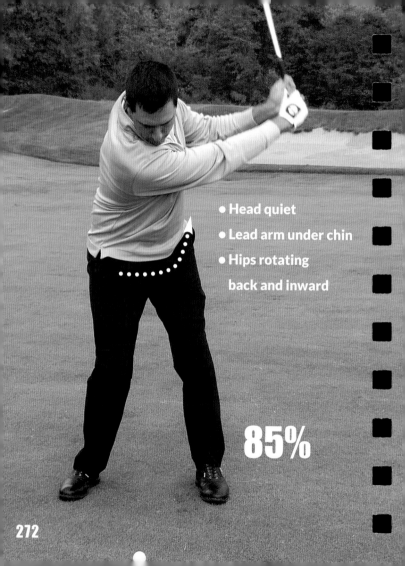

- Head quiet
- Lead arm under chin
- Hips rotating back and inward

85%

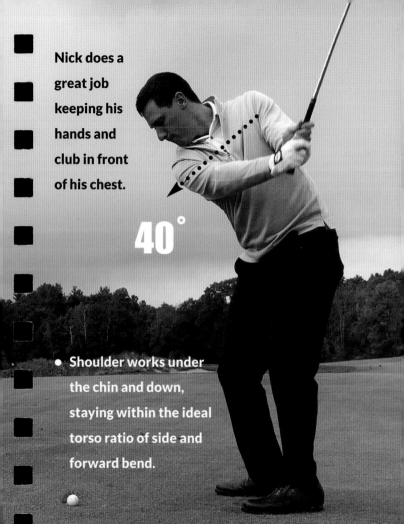

Nick does a great job keeping his hands and club in front of his chest.

40°

- Shoulder works under the chin and down, staying within the ideal torso ratio of side and forward bend.

273

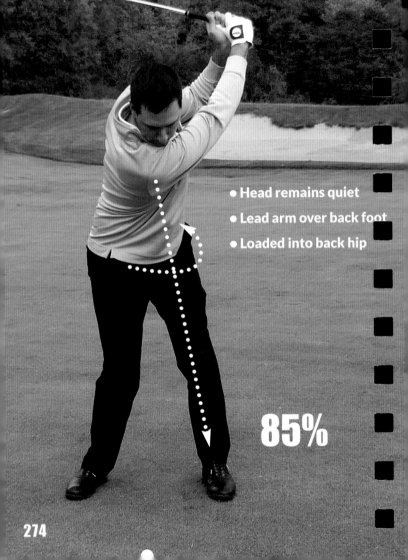

- Head remains quiet
- Lead arm over back foot
- Loaded into back hip

85%

274

good wrist angles

- Lead arm in line with shoulder with trail elbow pointing down

275

PRESSURE LEAN IN TO FRONT SIDE

- Entire lead side leans forward, moving pressure from back to lead side. Upper body rotation is passive with no hip rotation, just yet

85%

- **Hands have begun their descent, as a reaction to the transfer to lead side**

277

- Driving into the lead side as the club drops in the slot

88%

278

• **Shaft bisecting arms, indicating club is on-plane**

● Square
shoulder line
indicating a
good angle of
attack

88%

280

● There's that "trail hand on top" that we saw during the takeaway

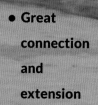

- Great connection and extension
- Head quiet

90%

DELIBERATE
STRIKE WITH FORCE

- Full extension keeping the clubhead low well past impact, maintaining posture
- Rotating his wrists for a power release

283

FOREARM
AND WRIST ROTATION

- Head remains still
- Forearm rotation producing tremendous clubhead speed

- Still in posture with hips fully cleared
- Club exiting at shoulder line

285

Standing tall and in perfect balance

95%

- **Fully vertical with trail shoulder and hip fully rotated right of the target in Nick's case (for a lefty)**
- **Back foot on toes**

DRIVER
KEY POINTS

- Neutral spine
- Weight pressure balls of feet
- Shoulders in line with toes
- Shaft of driver pointing to belt line

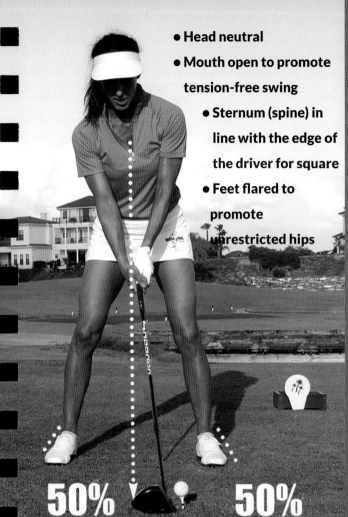

- Head neutral
- Mouth open to promote tension-free swing
- Sternum (spine) in line with the edge of the driver for square
- Feet flared to promote unrestricted hips

50% **50%**

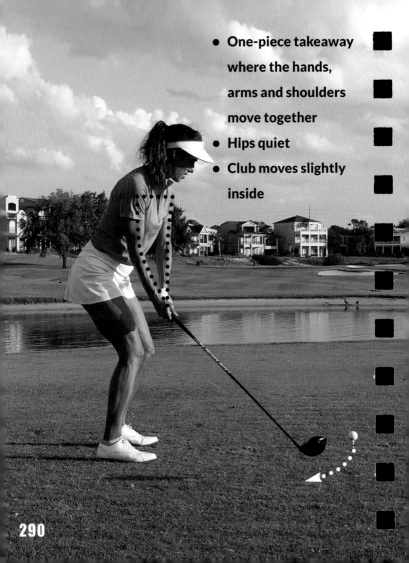

- **One-piece takeaway where the hands, arms and shoulders move together**
- **Hips quiet**
- **Club moves slightly inside**

- **Clubhead stays low during takeaway**
- **Pressure moves to back leg**

80%

TAKEAWAY
SQUARE AND WIDE

● **Clubface angle mirrors spine, indicating that it is square**

• Creating good
width at this stage
of the takeaway

• Pressing at an angle down into ground,
to rotate torso and stabilize the back leg

293

- Clubface mirrors lead arm, indicating a square clubface.
- Lead arm inline with shoulder, indicating on plane

294

90°

- Lead shoulder over back foot, indicating a full turn
- Hips rotated less than shoulder, indicating good power ratio

45°

- Back leg continuing to press at an angle into the ground

PASSIVE
CHEST DURING TRANSITION

- During the transition, the primary goal is moving pressure from the back side to front side

- The shaft angle has not changed as the hands drop down slightly, in reaction to the pressure move to the lead side

- **Moving pressure into lead leg at an angle toward front toe, as my back remains passive**

75%

297

- **Hips rotated, as chest remains square to target line**
- **Hands close to body to allow the clubhead to swing in to out**

- Lead arm pinned to chest indicating a good downswing. sequence. The lead arm will leverage the lead chest to whip the club past the body

299

- Hips rotated, more than chest just after impact
- Back foot on toes, indicating good transfer of pressure from back to front side

300

- Lead shoulder higher than trail, to promote launch
- Head passive to allow arms and club to whip by

301

RELEASE
IS LIGHTNING FAST

- **Trail hand parallel to target line**

THIGH TO THIGH

- Trail hand now on top, indicating a good release of the club

- My neck is not as mobile as Nick's, so I am allowing it to rotate toward the target

FULLY FINISH

ROTATED AWAY FROM THE TARGET

A complete finish keeps your clubhead speed elevated, optimizing ball speed.

- On toes indicating full pressure transfer to front side, allowing a full rotation well left of the target

- **Tall and balanced**
- **Back shoulder fully rotated**

90%

Head to MorePars.com to explore Christina's Iron and Wood Key Points!

TAKE ACTION

305

5 LOWER POWER MODIFICATIONS

5 POWER SWING LOWER BODY modifications to generate lots more clubhead speed

1. LEAD HEEL LIFTED DURING BACKSWING

provides a bigger backswing.

2. BIG WEIGHT SHIFT DURING BACKSWING

creates max ground force during downswing, but requires weight shift back.

3. JUMP!

adds a vertical thrust through impact.

4. BENT KNEE THROUGH IMPACT

helps stabilize rotary forces, creates a more shallow approach, and acts as a shock absorber.

5. SPINNING LEAD FOOT ON DOWNSWING

opens up lead side for more speed.

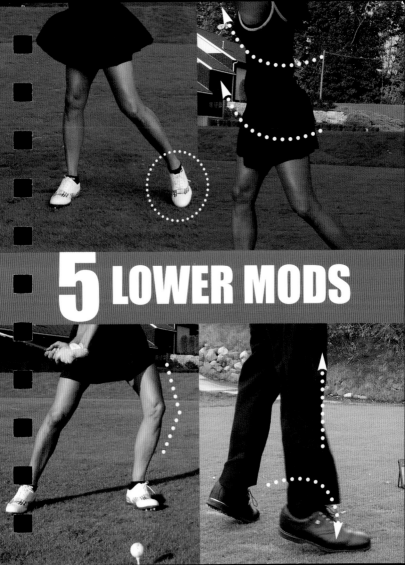

5 LOWER MODS

3 UPPER POWER MODIFICATIONS

3 POWER SWING UPPER BODY modifications
to generate lots more clubhead speed

1. HANDS AND ARMS HIGH

maximizes opportunity for

arm-chop power.

2. LEAD ARM BENT

adds another power lever.

3. FOREARM ROTATION

increases club axial rotation for

more club speed.

3 UPPER MODS

LIFT LEAD HEEL
DURING BACKSWING

Players who have limited mobility in their thoracic or have internal hip limitations can benefit from lifting the lead heel. In fact, many top players lift their lead heel during the backswing. Lifting the lead heel has these benefits:

• Increase downswing separation
• Allow for bigger backswing
• Easier to get hands high
• Trigger to initiate downswing

LOAD UP

DURING BACKSWING

The World Long Drive Hitters really load up on their trail side. They know that a big weight transfer equals lots of distance. Loading up during the backswing has these benefits:

- Increase downswing separation
- Allow for bigger backswing
- Easier to get hands high
- More mass to transfer to lead side

90%

VERTICAL JUMP

DURING DOWNSWING

The World Long Drive Hitters capitalize on the power of the vertical jump through the ball. In fact, they often jump as high as 5 inches off the ground through impact. A vertical jump has these benefits:

- Increase clubhead speed
- Helps with sequence
- Gets player more athletic
- Helps transfer pressure to lead side

4" UP

LEAD FOOT SPIN

ROTATE OPEN THROUGH IMPACT

The World Long Drive Hitters are great examples of how to hit the ball really far. For most of these players, the lead foot is off the ground and spun open (externally rotated). This foot action has these benefits:

- Allows for faster rotation
- Allows for full transfer of weight
- Great for players with lead ankle or hips limitations

318

BENT KNEE
THROUGH IMPACT

As students, we are taught to post up on the lead side...and this is true. However, many long hitters keep that lead knee flexed through the ball, which can have these benefits:

• Absorbs rotary force

• Promote an upward attack angle

• Shallows the approach for launch

• Note: Not recommended for players with knee limitations.

FLYING ELBOW

DURING BACKSWING

With traditional instruction, we are taught not to flare the trail elbow outward and to keep hands far away from our head during the backswing. However, if we look at some of the longest ball strikers, their hands are high, close to their head, and their elbows are flaring outward. This type of backswing has these benefits:

• Decrease inertia for faster rotary speed

• Allows for bigger backswing

• Easier to get hands high

• Increases Chop Power

When shopping drivers, ask about head design sizes and options. Options available will be based on your clubhead speed, path and attack angle. There are also options for a draw, straight or fade bias shot. Techy? Explore the adjustable heads too!

TAKE ACTION

Head to MorePars.com to explore this Power Equipment section!

EXPLORE MORE BOOKS!

GETMOREPARS.COM

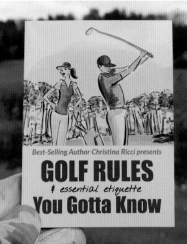

INCLUDES
MOST COMMON RULES:
STAKES
UNPLAYABLES
CART PATH
AND MORE MORE
+ IMPLEMENTS THE
2019 MAJOR RULES CHANGES

EASY-TO-FOLLOW • PERFECTLY SIZE
FOR ALL PLAYERS • RETAIL $15.95

BENT ELBOW

AT TOP OF BACKSWING

Many World Long Drive Hitters
bend their trail arm at the top of the
backswing because they know it has a few
key speed benefits:

- Adds another lever to the chain
- Decreases inertia (hands closer to head)
- Increases rotary power on downswing
- Helps to get hands higher for
  more chop power

FOREARMS
POST-IMPACT

The money shot! Yep. We see it on the covers of top golf magazines. It's the famous Forearm Release. This power rotation creates tremendous extra clubhead speed. In fact, there is a misconception that one needs to keep the clubface facing the target for as long as possible. This is fine for accuracy, but will decrease club and ball speed. You can enjoy plenty of accuracy with shorter clubs into the green for more GIRs.

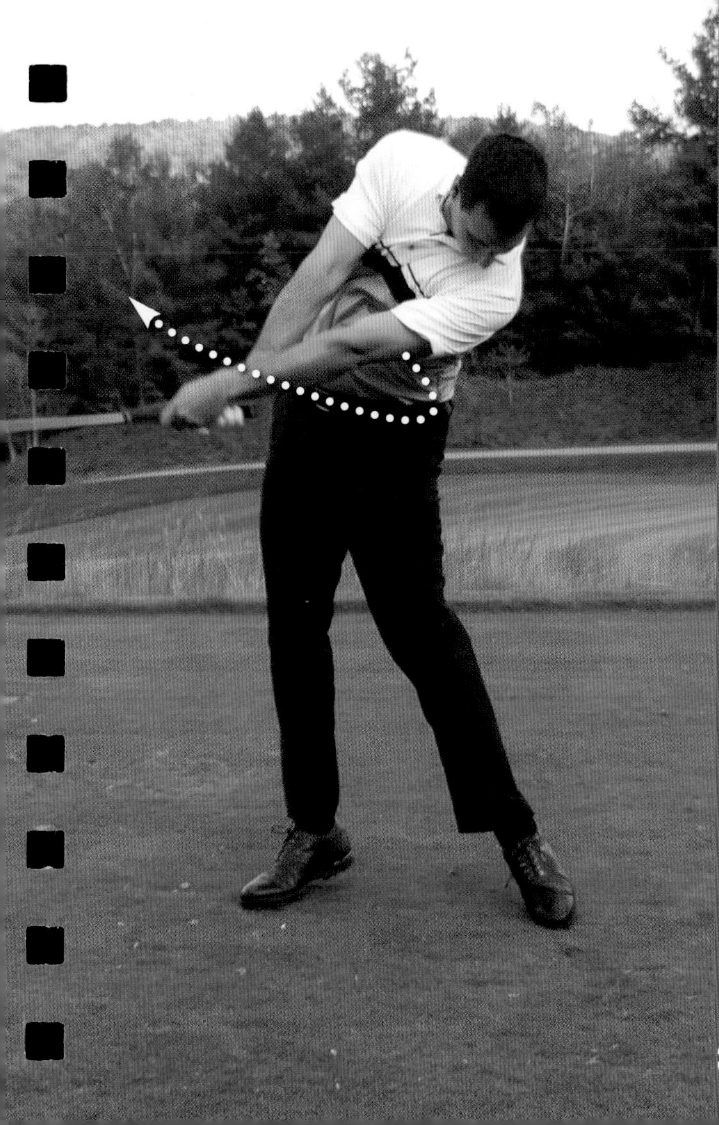

SWING STRATEGIES FOR
PHYSICAL LIMITATIONS

For everyday golfers, playing at an elite tour level is not a realistic scenario. The majority spend long periods sitting at a desk, commuting to work and raising a family. Plus, the golf swing is very demanding physically. Tight or de-conditioned muscles will affect our efficiency on the course. So what are you to do? The first step is to assess the situation. The next step is to work toward a solution.

TAKE ACTION

Head to MorePars.com to explore this awesome section!

POWER EQUIPMENT

SECTION III MORE PARS POWER

POWER
EQUIPMENT

Inside this section

- Equipment Overview
- Shaft Variables
- Loft, COG & MOI
- Grip Size is a Big Deal
- 10 Things to Know About Irons
- 10 Buying Tips
- Club Yardages & Loft

When it comes to getting more distance and more greens in regulations, a player must understand the incredible influence their equipment has on center-face contact. That's the name of the ball striking game. Optimize your body, technique and equipment to optimize center-face contact, repeatedly. In fact, consistency is the number one request from my students and YouTube viewers.

The first place to look are your clubs. In this section, you'll learn the important equipment variables for drivers and irons. Clubs play a significant role in ball flight, distance and feel. When a club is properly fitted, the swing has the best chance of being efficient. Clubs that are not fitted may result in a player having to alter the swing (consciously or subconsciously) to make contact with the ball. The clubs also need to "look good" from the player's perspective. Clubs provide confidence and more pars when properly fitted for your size, strength, skill level and swing characteristics.

So, let's get to it!

UNDERSTANDING CLUB VARIABLES

Understanding all the variables that encompass your equipment, specifically your driver and irons, will help you be a better student...and a better player. Compatible equipment is paramount for more pars.

VARIABLES THAT YOU'LL LEARN:

- Static vs Dynamic Measurements
- Club Length, Weight & Material
- Lie Angle (irons, hybrids)
- Shaft Flex   • COG & MOI
- Driver Loft   • Grip Size
- Filling the Gaps - Club Yardages